Bittersweet Memories

PARUL NIGAM

Notion Press

Old No. 38, New No. 6
McNichols Road, Chetpet
Chennai - 600 031

First Published by Notion Press 2020
Copyright © Parul Nigam 2020
All Rights Reserved.

ISBN 978-1-64828-759-6

Unheard words
of an eighteen year old girl.
A tale of joy, pain, love and healing.

ACKNOWLEDGEMENTS

Baba, you would've been proud of me
if you were here.
We miss you.

Thanks to every single person who encouraged me and supported me in writing this book, mom for always believing in me and helping me chase my dreams, dada for guiding me through out the process and dad for making them come true. Rishabh, thank you for being a constant source of hope and inspiration. My best friend, Nimit, thank you for making me laugh when I was struggling with writer's block and my mentor and best friend Prashuk, thank you for constantly motivating me, without you I would not have become the writer I am today. Thanks to my fellow poets of Instagram who supported me at every step and the people who helped indirectly with this book, I am eternally grateful to all of you.

I am also thankful to everyone who has ever walked out of my life, you are one of the reasons how this book came into existence.

FROM THE AUTHOR

To the tender hands who are holding my heart,

thank you for choosing me,
thank you for letting me in,
thank you for making me stay.

For once just forget who you are, and feel my heart in your warm palms trying to recite an unheard tale, trying to tell you the extent to which a young heart can feel, trying to tell you that no matter what the world says, you know what's inside, you know what you face every day behind those curtains of fear.

They've always said,
"You are too young to feel this way"

and I have always replied,
"You won't understand"

When the pain made my lips numb
then my fingers started bleeding words.

You are too young to write
about love and hate,
but age is just a number
don't they say?
I have felt it all
no less than an adult
then why do they ask me
to not speak, to stay hush.
I lower my voice,
they say quiet
you are too naive,
too young to interrupt,
and I am silenced.
Yet again.

I feel power
in my finger tips
in this pen
in my words

they are
my weapons
and I'll use them

slowly
carefully

to heal you
on the inside.

You chain your feet with fears
and then complain
why you can't walk forward.

My dreams were never too small
to be caged inside four walls.

What more are we but broken hearts
chasing and blaming love.

We search for peace
in every storm
and expect a rainbow
after every rain,
forgetting the nature
of the world
that beauty resides
at times
in feeling pain.

You are so much more
than what they made you think of yourself.

If these walls could speak,
they would have told you
the story of my pain,
since they have heard me
breaking at half past twelve,
only if these walls could speak
they would have told you,
it wasn't easy for me
and therefore
it won't be for you.

Don't let the mirror force you
to become something you're not.

My heart feels so heavy,
as if it's tied
with chains and anchors,
like the roots hanging down
from a banyan tree.
I'm drowning slowly
in a puddle of melancholy.
I can hear it screaming
for help
and begging
for healing.
But here I am,
even after knowing
everything,
even after knowing
no one can heal it but me
I do nothing

-whose fault?

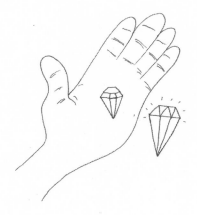

In search of a forever,
you will lose your today.

They have always said to us women,
"Don't compare yourself with men"
"Don't compare yourself with men"
"Don't compare yourself with men"

I guess they were right.
Men use dominance as their weapon,
to satisfy their ego, their superiority.
But we women, use patience and kindness,
and sometimes even suffocate our peace.

For so many years
tolerance has been the core force,
otherwise some relations
would have been broken long ago
because men don't have that courage
to face the rage and fire
that burns inside a woman's chest.

Turn ice cold,
wear a mask of strength,
pretend you're okay
and the weakness
does not exist,

but think of becoming fire
that burns everything down,
everything that comes in its way,

wait for the right time
one stroke is enough
to ignite, to make everything,
everything your prey.

My home is a place that is messy but beautiful. It smells of my dreams and achievements, the windows are covered with hopes and expectations. Bird of peace comes and sits at the little niche that is at the front wall of the entrance. I have decorated it with beautiful portraits of myself at every stage of life. I have the finest memories from all around the world kept safely inside and pieces of myself carved into the most exquisite shapes that could possibly exist. I am the queen here, with or without a king. Every morning I breathe sunshine mixed with hope, I look into the mirror, take a sip from my coffee and remind myself about the beauty that resides inside, about the uniqueness that can not be found anywhere else in the world. I tell myself that I am the most powerful person here and therefore I must value myself and my opinions. No stranger or outsider has the power to destroy it; none. This is my home and the only one who is in charge of whatever happens here is me.

The master
was once a beginner,
the beginner
will be a master someday.

O dear novice,
don't let anyone
convince you
that you can't do it.

Neither the master,
nor you yourself.

I looked into the mirror,
these scars made me hate this skin,
beneath it,
I am just blood and bones,
like you, like her
and like him.
What makes me different from you,
this colour? these scars?
what makes me inferior
when inside there's just another heart.

This body, my body,
is not meant for judgements.
I must not be ashamed
wearing my own skin.
It is meant to be treasured
the way it is,
I must embrace
each and every memory
that lingers on it.

A world that is trying to make you somebody else, where people are trying to paint you with colours of their choice, where there are strangers ready with moulds in their hands wanting to take away your uniqueness and pour you into a container that does not belong to you. My warrior, I see you and I am glad that you are still fighting and I am sure that someday you'll win this tug of war. How strong are you I wonder, to fight for your identity. Stay there, don't let them paint you or carve you into a sculpture that you aren't meant to be, don't let them decorate you with ornaments that people have already used. I want you to keep adoring your shades. The beauty that defines you, the universe that resides inside you, I want you to embrace your individuality until the end.

It's hard to let go
when you still have hope.

I don't know how it feels
to not feel in extremes,

to not give too much,
to not take too much,
to not be too much,

I don't know
how to be nothing
while being
everything.

The flame of love ignites once,
and with every wind
of insecurity and doubt
it grows smaller

until one day
it fades away.

It's tiring
to give and give,
and
love and love,
for how long can you
extract water from a river
that receives no rain?

We search for the best
at all the worst places.

You never cared for the love
only wanted the attention,

I was naive
and in a misconception.

You wanted to touch my wings
but refused to feel the claws,

I still hoped that one day
you would embrace my flaws.

Love, my dear, has the power to heal
every inch of your aching heart.

Stop hiding your scars
from people who caused them,

stop searching for love
in empty promises,

stop apologizing for mistakes
you intentionally never did,

stop expecting the return
of the people who left,

stop begging for someone
to stay in your life,

stop being afraid to ask
for things that are yours,

stop denying things
that you want
and learn to say no
to the things that you don't.

Caged by your own demons
you tell me I am not free
well, I guess you never noticed
the chains tied to your feet.

Sadly, it takes ages
for lovers like us

to first fall in love

and then
fall out of it.

I want you to know
that forever exists,
it's just hiding
behind those curtains
of doubts and fears.

Love my scars
and heart,
not just my skin.

In return,
I'll surrender
my naked soul
to you.

You are making me addicted
to your love like wine,
I drown a little more
each time I taste it.

You hold that knife
too close to your chest
and try to explain yourself
that it is okay to bleed
for people you love,

that is where I'll stop you
and remind you it's not
to treat your heart too carelessly
as if it's nothing but dust.

You should know when to walk away, even if it breaks your heart, even if it's the last thing you would wish to do, you should know when you must. People out there are cruel, some of them won't mind ripping your heart apart for their own selfish needs. I know it sounds terrible, but if I break it down to you, people won't think twice before cutting you off if it's for their own good. The world has changed, relations aren't so pure the way they used to be, and you never know who would come when, with a needle to puncture your little bubble of happiness.

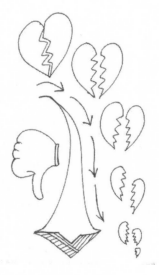

Know your worth before people define it.

I took away everything
from your hands
after seeing
how careless you were
with precious things

but sadly I forgot
that my heart
could someday
be counted
as one of them.

You don't realise
love is like a bullet
until it hits right in
your chest too hard.
You don't realise
people aren't homes
until they walk away
and abandon your heart.

Stop forcing it on time,
time cannot fix your broken pieces.

You are the rose
by whose thorns
I would love to bleed.

No matter how hard you try
a desolate place
won't yield a thing,

if a person doesn't care for you,
they never have,
then they never will.

I give myself false hopes
someday you will come back to me
apologize for what you did
and accept your faults
that earlier you refused to see.

How sad this is,
that day would never come
and this hope will never go.

He was like wine,
and I tell you,
I've never been sober
since I've tasted him.

Words work like bandages
on our wounded hearts

-and sometimes
they rip our chests apart.

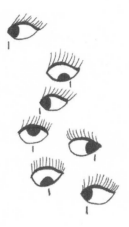

I want you to want me too,
I want you to need me too,
it feels like every time I fall in love
it is with the wrong person.

I am tired of feeling this,
this unrequited love,
it makes me feel invisible.

Some of us move on,

some of us surrender
and learn to live with it,

unlucky are those
who can't do either.

'Good-byes' are hard,

the ones
that aren't said
are harder

and the ones
we don't want to say
are the hardest to face.

But how do I explain it
to this wild thing
caged between my ribs
that you would
never return home?

You won't love me for my sins,
if the stories inside my heart
appeared on my skin.

Like fools we chase
things that we love,
so blindly, so recklessly
that we agree
to burn for them
without any hesitation.

If the earth can appear
to meet the sky
at the horizon
then maybe
in a parallel universe
'we' exist too.

He broke me into a million pieces,
I still went to him to fix me up.

RISE LIKE A PHOENIX

We listen to the things
people keep on saying
and then
start to believe
it is the only truth.

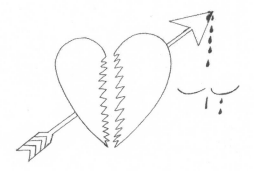

Dear heart,
I want you to stop waiting
for the thing that was never yours.

Lonely nights will teach you
the necessity of self love.

Our paths crossed,
the universe wanted us
to meet,
but that definitely
did not mean
that we were
meant to be.

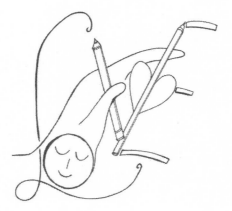

These words, they healed me,
they will heal you too.

Finally you opened the door
and let me inside your heart,
I felt suffocated
to see it on the inside.

A place that I longed to be in
for so many years,
was so dark and desolate
that it made me pity
its existence.

-you never know what's inside

Bloom, bloom in front of me,
open your petals one by one,
and let me adore you
for whatever you are,
for the rest of your life.

My stars don't match with your stars,
we are two separate galaxies.

Love needs patience to grow
and perseverance to keep growing.

I will give you my heart
right in your hands
but I am not sure
that they won't tremble
with the fear of trying
to love something
so full of love already.

All I ever asked you
was to stay with me,

all you ever wanted
was the permission
to leave.

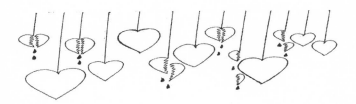

Allow yourself
to heal completely
before opening the doors
of your heart again.

Someone is there
somewhere in the world
who will listen.

They will weep with you
and hear your screams,
just like these pages you hide
under your pillow at 2 a.m.
when someone knocks the door,
they will keep your secrets
safe in their hearts.

They will understand,
before being understood.

Don't kill your peace
for someone
who is always ready
to begin a war
inside you.

Love will never ask you
to surrender your self respect.

Wounds take time to heal,
especially the ones
which have been there for years.

You are allowed to cry rivers
while longing for someone,
while healing from pain
given by love,
but you must not forget
to hold your heart
to such an extent,
that you do not drown
in your own flood.

He touches me like the waves touch the shore,
taking away a part of me each time.

We are fools to chase the ones
who were never meant to stay.

Believe me or not,
but the sad memories
don't fade away.

Neither with time
nor on their own.

Your memories haunt me more than anything,
more than any lover ever has and ever will,
more than the demons inside my head,
more than the sweet divine love itself.

You are my moon,
and the wolf in me howls every night for you.

It takes time to grow flowers again,
when you've been growing thorns for too long.

Now that you are here,
now that I am yours,
I hope you are not
just another man
who is here
for a vacation
or just for the cover page.
I hope you are not here
for my eyes, for my voice
or for the way I laugh.
I hope you are not here
to hurt my petals
or scratch my wounds.

I hope you are here
because you want to be
and I hope
you love me for me
and not for what you see.

Don't hold too tight,
it will all slip away like sand any moment.

I hope your heart
does not ache
when you think of love,
I hope you receive it
in such abundance
that you never
have to long for it
when it's not around.

I love you
with all of my broken heart,
every single piece
has your name
carved on them,

little sculptures
reference of pain.

Sometimes staying apart is wiser
than staying together
and killing each other.

I hope your heart
falls in love too hard
and safely land into hands
that offer all the love in the world.

The flowers in my garden still smell like you.

If the universe grants me a wish
I would ask for a forever,
where time doesn't exist
and the spring never leaves,
where our love could bloom wildly
with the things that never sleep,
where we could forever be
in each other's sight
and there's no lonely day to come
when the sun doesn't shine.

Since I have survived your loss,
I know I can survive anything now.

You left,

while I was lying there
helplessly
on the floor

that day
was the end of you
and the beginning of me.

If only the stars could see
what a beauty you are,
they would fall in love with you
instead of the moon.

Never be afraid to start again.

I am a one man army. I try to fix the bullet holes myself because I've realized that the wounds will heal only if I let them. I am the sole body that holds the responsibility of the bad things that happen. I am a warrior and now I know how to survive. I have seen people change like seasons. But now the directions have changed, I am brave, I am the lioness and this is my land. I must slaughter anyone who takes me for nothing, and roar so loud that even the mountains come down to their feet because I am no longer the wind, but the raging storm.

Let my fingers dance on these pages again,
let me pour my soul out before it's too late,
let my heart break once again,

But I still won't stop believing
that the sun would shine again.

In the blink of an eye,
the dream melts in your mouth like sugar,
and there's nothing in the world
you can do to live it again.

For god's sake,
don't think I am weak.
I am not that woman anymore,

who would bend down to her knees
just to please you,
who would obey your orders like a slave,
who would let herself be your prey,

and you like a vulture
would rip her flesh open
and scrape her from head to toe
unless your hunger is satisfied,

sorry not sorry,
I am not that woman anymore.

This time,
let the love be wild,
for the world
is quite good
at hurting things
that are soft.

She isn't afraid
to start destruction
in the blink of an eye,
or burn a place
down with her rage,
don't try to cage her
in bars or boundaries
for she will melt them
and escape.

We all are either longing for something
or healing from something.

You don't need them love,
you don't need someone
who left you burning in pain.

I'll carve the broken pieces of yours,
paint them with love and care,
sprinkle stardust on them
and a lot more respect for yourself,

then I'll join them
together,
carefully,
to show you,
you are no less
than a masterpiece.

I have seen deaths
of so many versions
of myself,
and I am ready to face
a thousand more
if that's what it takes
to become
what I am meant to be.

My wings aren't broken,
it's just the resting phase.

My passion
to achieve
my dreams
grows everyday
like wildfire.

No rain
of comfort
can stop me
from burning
the grass of
criticism
and hate.

For you,
I would have done
anything in the world,

but in return
you would have
given me nothing

except sleepless nights
and endless hurt.

Notice the way
he touches your skin,
if he loves you
then you will feel the love
dripping from his fingertips.

You don't deserve a 'somewhat' or 'almost' type of love, you deserve a fairytale ending, a together forever kind of story. Don't let your love be mediocre and don't settle for mediocre love. Someone is out there, searching for a lover like you, craving for a love like yours. Don't settle, life is too short to stay unhappy with things you can control. Love will come to you, if not, then it will definitely find you, but when it's the right time. You may not find love when you're searching for it with open arms but you will surely find it when you're expecting it the least.

Pain has the power to evolve you
into an exquisite masterpiece.

As I saw the dry leaf falling down,
I thought about moments,
the bad ones,
the ones that made me what I am today,
the way it fell down
the same way we let go of the toxics,
to evolve and to move ahead
from people, feelings and memories,
which make us vulnerable and weak,
and threaten the peace of our inner selves.

Then, I saw the banyan tree,
still and calm, tall and firm.
I wonder, I wonder
how strong it would be.

Every time I saw it,
it gave me reminders,
reminders to be powerful.

No matter how hard the time is,
I could rise and start again.
No matter how hard I hit the ground
I can learn to fly again.

To all the broken souls out there, and to the people who are bravely fighting battles of their lives, this one is for you.

I hope that the universe guides you home
each time you feel lost.
I hope that you gather courage
to fight the battles that come your way.
I hope that the things fall back
into their places soon.
I hope that the sun shines
when you're having your darkest days.

There will be days when you'll wake up hating yourself and nights when you'll be in utter distress. There will be days when you will question your worth, and believe whatever your demons will feed your head. There will be days when suicidal thoughts will linger in your mind, and nothing in the world would seem fine. But trust me, even the darkest nights come to an end.

The pain will evolve you, the lessons will make you wiser, the hurt will make you stronger, and it will all eventually make you a fighter. Vulnerability, empathy, tears aren't mere signs of weakness. Some people feel more than others and that's okay. A thousand deaths can't stop you from rising again, my phoenix, die a thousand deaths, but each time rise, rise and be better, stronger, wiser and purer from before. Amidst the dark be your own source of light. I know you can do this, because you did not come this far to let 'any' human break your heart.

ABOUT THE AUTHOR

Parul started writing when she was 15, soon after that she started sharing it on Instagram to reach out to the people who were in pain or going through tough times. She wanted her posts to be a harbinger of hope and strength to every person who thought of themselves as depressed or weak. She is an avid reader and a deep thinker, she loves singing and exploring new fields of knowledge. She believes that age should not define the extent to which a human being can feel and people like her need to express themselves in order to keep themselves sane, thus she strongly recommends writing for those who often overthink. She hails from Kanpur, Uttar Pradesh and is pursuing her bachelor in arts from Hyderabad, you can connect to her @theenchantedgirl on Instagram.